Older, Wiser...
Sexier

OLDER, WISER... SEXIER

Summersdale Publishers Ltd
46 West Street
Chichester
West Sussex
PO19 1RP
UK

www.summersdale.com

Printed and bound in China

ISBN: 978-1-84953-019-4

Substantial discounts on bulk quantities of Summersdale books are available to corporations, professional associations and other organisations. For details contact Summersdale Publishers by telephone: +44 (0) 1243771107, fax: +44 (0) 1243 786300 or email: nicky@summersdale.com.

Older, Wiser...
Sexier

Bev Williams

Age is a question of mind over matter. If you don't mind, it doesn't matter!

Mark Twain

Eventually you will reach a point when you stop lying about your age and start bragging about it.

Will Rogers

Older, wiser...

sexier.

Men are like wine. Some turn to vinegar, but the best improve with age.
C. E. M. Joad

Getting old is a bit like getting drunk; everyone else looks brilliant.
Billy Connolly

If in doubt...

add more wine.

If you resolve to give up smoking, drinking and loving, you don't actually live longer. It just seems longer.

Clement Freud

I want to have a good body, but not as much as I want dessert.

Jason Love

I used to think I'd like less grey hair. Now I'd like more of it.

Richie Benaud

I knew I was going bald when it was taking me longer and longer to wash my face.

Harry Hill

It's a huge responsibility –

being the ultimate fantasy pin-up.

Don't worry about temptation.
As you grow older, it
starts avoiding you.

Winston Churchill

Advanced old age is when you sit
in a rocking chair and you can't
get it going.

Eliakim Katz

'You want me to come upstairs and
make love to you?

It will have to be one or the other.'

My doctor told me to watch my drinking, so I now do it in front of the mirror.

Rodney Dangerfield

One Martini is all right. Two are too many, and three are not enough.

James Thurber

For us elderly people, not owning a computer is like not having a headache.

Edward Enfield

What do gardeners do
when they retire?

Bob Monkhouse

Old gardeners don't die. They just
throw in the trowel.

Audrey Austin

'Now don't worry. I
promise not to plan...

a garden bigger than
you can look after.'

The older you get the more
important it is not to act your age.

Ashleigh Brilliant

Middle age is when you're old
enough to know better but still
young enough to do it.

Ogden Nash

'Today is the day I show the world
what living is all about...

I'll wear my jersey inside out!'

Just remember, once you're over the hill, you begin to pick up speed.

Charles M. Schulz

They say the first thing to go when you're old is your legs or your eyesight. It isn't true. The first thing to go is parallel parking.

Kurt Vonnegut

To a man who has everything going for him.

Eyes going, teeth going, hearing going...

One of the many things
nobody tells you about
middle age is that it's a nice
change from being young.

William Feather

The best part of the art of living is
to know how to grow old gracefully.

Eric Hoffer

'I think our children should have all the things we didn't have...

and then we'll move in with them.'

The problem with the world is that
everyone is a few drinks behind.

Humphrey Bogart

The best birthdays are all those that
haven't arrived yet.

Robert Orben

To a man who knows –

how to behave himself.

A man has reached
middle age when he is
advised to slow down
by his doctor rather
than the police.

Anonymous

My wife said to me, 'I don't look 50, do I darling?' I said 'Not anymore.'

Bob Monkhouse

I just tell people I'm as old as my wife. Then I lie about her age.

Fred Metcalf

'We have been married for many years and never once considered divorce...

murder yes, divorce no.'

That outdoor grilling is a manly pursuit has long been beyond question.

William Geist

Red meat is not bad for you. Now blue-green meat, that's bad for you!

Tommy Smothers

Man's last great challenge –

The Summer Barbecue.

As for me, except for an occasional heart attack, I feel as young as I ever did.

Robert Benchley

Middle age is the time when a man is always thinking in a week or two he will feel as good as ever.

Don Marquis

True happiness is knowing...

someone thinks you're a star.

Burgundy makes you think of
silly things, Bordeaux makes
you talk of them and Champagne
makes you do them.

Jean-Anthelme Brillat-Savarin

Good wine is a necessity of life for me.

Thomas Jefferson

When a recipe says 'add wine',

never ask 'to what?'

When a man retires his wife
gets twice the husband but
only half the income.

Chi Chi Rodriguez

I don't want to retire. I'm not that
good at crossword puzzles.

Norman Mailer

Men chase golf balls
when they're too old to
chase anything else.

Groucho Marx

'He's punishing his clubs...

because they played so badly!'

Middle age is when you
are not inclined to exercise
anything but caution.

Arthur Murray

To win back my youth... there is
nothing I wouldn't do – except take
exercise, get up early, or be a useful
member of the community.

Oscar Wilde

Back in the 60s we turned on,
tuned in and dropped out.

Now we tune in, turn
over and drop off.

Jameson's Irish Whiskey really does improve with age: the older I get the more I like it.

Bob Monkhouse

I like my whiskey old and my women young.

Errol Flynn

Growing old is compulsory,
growing up is optional.

Bob Monkhouse

You are only young once, but you
can be immature for a lifetime.

John P. Grier

At your age people expect you to be calm, dignified and sober.

Disappoint them.

I'm getting to an age when I can enjoy the last sport left. It is called hunting for your spectacles.

Edward Grey

When you become senile, you won't know it.

Bill Cosby

'I've just been for a long walk in the countryside. I'm not much of a walker –

but I can't remember where I left my car.'

Boys will be boys and so will a lot of middle-aged men.

Kin Hubbard

Experience is a comb life gives you after you lose your hair.

Judith Stern

Inside every mature person
is an immature person shouting:

'What the hell happened?'

One of the good things
about getting older is
that you find you're more
interesting than most of
the people you meet.
Lee Marvin

If only we were all...

as gifted, talented and as good
looking as you.

Don't let ageing get you down. It's too hard to get back up.

John Wagner

I have the body of an 18-year-old. I keep it in the fridge.

Spike Milligan

'On the whole, the years have been kind to us all.

It was just the weekends that did the damage.'

They say that age is all in your mind. The trick is keeping it from creeping down into your body.

Anonymous

Wrinkles should merely indicate where smiles have been.

Mark Twain

As you grow older,
your nose drops...

thank God nothing else does.

When they tell me I'm too old
to do something, I attempt it
immediately.

Pablo Picasso

No man is ever old enough
to know better.

Holbrook Jackson

Feeling older...

is for sissies.

As you get older three things happen. The first is your memory goes, and I can't remember the other two...

Norman Wisdom

First, you forget names, then you forget faces. Next, you forget to pull your zipper up and finally you forget to pull it down.

Leo Rosenberg

'No no – I don't want a floral fantasy tattooed up my arm.

I just want my address, my pin numbers, and oh yes – my name.'

We don't grow older, we grow riper.

Pablo Picasso

Live each day as if it were
your last, and garden as
though you will live forever.

Anonymous

Growing older?

No – you just need re-potting.

Always do sober what you said you'd do when you were drunk. That will teach you to keep your mouth shut!

Charles Scribner Jr

Save water –

drink wine.

When people tell you how young
you look they are also telling you
how old you are.

Cary Grant

When it comes to staying young, a
mind-lift beats a facelift any day.

Marty Bucella

When you look in the mirror, you see...

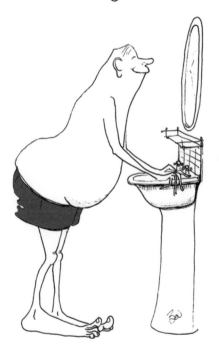

a very slim and very wise young person.

They tell you that you'll lose your mind when you grow older. What they don't tell you is that you won't miss it very much.

Malcolm Cowley

By the time you're eighty years old you've learned everything. You only have to remember it.

Bill Vaughan

'Is it time for your
medication, or mine?'

You know you've reached middle-age when your weightlifting consists merely of standing up.

Bob Hope

Now I'm over 50 my doctor says I should go out and get more fresh air and exercise. I said, 'All right, I'll drive with the car window open.'

Angus Walker

You can't help getting older, but
you don't have to get old.

George Burns

When you are dissatisfied and
would like to go back to your youth,
think of algebra.

Will Rogers

Both you and the wine
improve with age...

and the more you age, the more we
love you.

I'd hate to die with a good liver, good kidneys and a good brain. When I die I want everything to be knackered.

Hamish Imlach

One of the advantages of being 70 is that you need only 4 hours' sleep. True, you need it 4 times a day, but still.

Denis Norden

You read about the dangers of
alcohol so you had better give up –

reading.

Old age likes indecency.
It's a sign of life.

Mason Cooley

I love a man with a bit of...

spice in his life.

Never be afraid to try
something new.

Bob Hope

And in the end, it's not the years in
your life that count. It's the life in
your years.

Abraham Lincoln

Live for the moment...

and never dance with boring people.

Have you enjoyed this book? If so, why not write a review on your favourite website?

Thanks very much for buying this Summersdale book.

www.summersdale.com

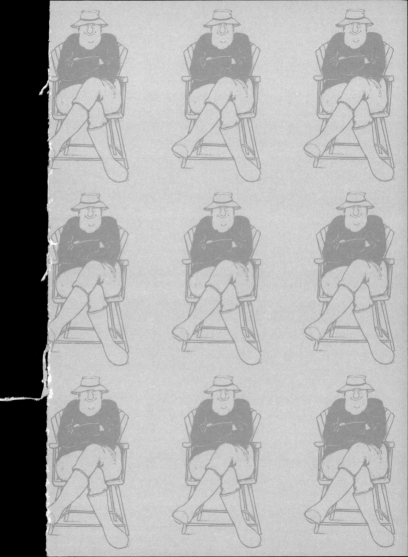

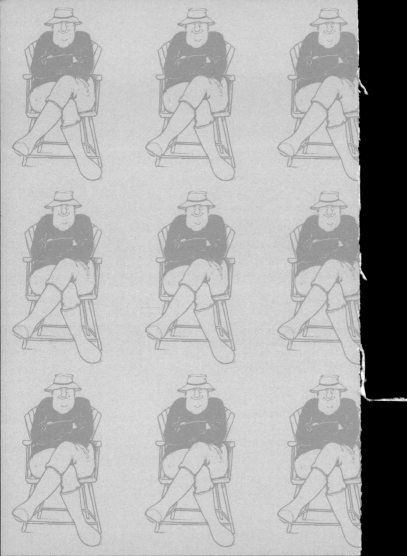